Whispers & Memoirs

Willette E. Mosby-Reynolds

authorHOUSE®

AuthorHouse™
1663 Liberty Drive
Bloomington, IN 47403
www.authorhouse.com
Phone: 1 (800) 839-8640

Published by AuthorHouse 10/31/2016

ISBN: 978-1-5246-4807-7 (sc)
ISBN: 978-1-5246-4806-0 (e)

"Author Willette Mosby-Reynolds has uniquely brought everyday life to the pages of her book and made known, with God's help, no matter what you are dealing with, you can succeed. Whispers & Memoirs is exciting, practical, transparent and written from a seat of experience. It captures the readers' attention and allows them to know, God, as the solution is always greater than even your worst of problems. Once I started reading, I did not put it down until conclusion and was left wanting more. All will leave motivated to live their lives to the fullest."

Dr. K.T. Lowery
Senior Pastor of Grace Church of Durham, North Carolina

Whispers

In quietness and in confidence
shall be your strength

A 7-day Meditation Devotional

Intro

It's a brand new day. Expect God to show up in some way. Look for Him. Listen. He's there and His delight is YOU. Appreciate the sunrise and sunset, the fresh air, the natural landscapes painted for our pleasure, the wind and even the rain.

For the next seven days, I'd like to share a special message with you. I pray that you are receptive and eager to hear what the Lord has to say.

Day ONE Topic: God Is the Strength of Our Life

Scripture:

> "But without faith it is impossible to please Him: for he that cometh to God must believe that He Is, and that He is a rewarder of those who diligently seek Him."
>
> Hebrews 11:6 KJV

Keywords: Believe. Rewarder. Diligently. Seek.

Message:

Yes, we know there is a God. I know without a shadow of doubt that there is. And we are familiar with some of His wonders or at least we've heard about them. Right? So the issue is not really believing that "He Is." Guess it could be hard to really feel that our majestic heavenly Father cares about little ole me and you. Believe it. He cares more than our earthly mother and father, and is able to do even more than we could ask, think or even imagine.

I encourage you to get into His Word and discover His promises, get to know Him, do everything as unto Him, and let your lifestyle speak of your relationship with Him. And because you are His, seeking Him, being a light on a hill and the salt of the earth, He in return will take care of you and shower you with His continuous blessings. We are healthy, intelligent, beautiful, kind-hearted & generous. We have been blessed with material possessions such as nice homes and cars. We are hard-working, dependable, people of integrity and great work ethic. We are peacemakers. We love the Lord! We have so much to be thankful for.

We should set high expectations for ourselves and also raise our expectations of God. The Word says that we are to believe that He will reward us. Expect great things. Expect even small things. Trust and believe that God cares, sees and will do for us.

Reward means we have done or will do something that warrants something good in return. Diligent means steady, earnest and energetic effort. Keep asking, believing, trusting, speaking those things that are not as though they were until it manifests. Then remember to show gratitude. THINK. ACT. EXPECT. Then THANK. We are going to stand like the Hebrew boys: We know that He is able to deliver us from every situation. But even if He doesn't, we will not bow to satan or any of his tricks, we refuse to give up [anything]. We stand boldly on His Word and choose to keep on trusting God. We are forever His.

Prayer:

Almighty God, in the name of your son, Jesus, we enter Your Presence with thanksgiving. Thank you, God, for who You Are and everything you do. Father, we appreciate your many blessings and we thank you for your written Word. We ask that you help us to live lives pleasing in your sight. We know that you are concerned about all that concerns us. You know all about us and what we each have need of; you know our heart's desires, our strengths and our shortcomings. And you love us just the same. Help us to obediently wait for your direction in all aspects of our lives. We love and adore you. And it is in the name of Jesus that we do pray. Amen.

Day TWO Topic: We Shall NOT Be Moved!

Scripture:

> "We are troubled on every side, yet not distressed; we are perplexed, but not in despair; persecuted, but not forsaken; cast down, but not destroyed"
>
> 2 Corinthians 4:8-9 KJV

Keyword: NOT.

Message:

This passage is so assuring and encouraging, to me. Though we may be in the midst of chaos all around us – home, work, church, with friends, with family, just life itself – all is NOT lost. There is a flip side. The present situation is NOT the end of our story. Because of Jesus and the price He paid for our salvation, NOT even death has power over us. Just think about that for a moment. Things are NOT always what they seem; appearances can be deceiving. Hold on to the Word of God. If you're knocked down, catch your breath and get up. Stand in the power of His might. Call upon the name of the Lord. God is our refuge and strength, a very present help in trouble.

In this short verse, the word "not" is declared four times. The point is well taken. God has the last say. It is not over until He says it's over. We will NOT quit, even when we feel as if we can't go another day. We may not understand. We may feel all alone. We may be confused or just not really sure. But deep within, we will find the strength to keep on keeping on. Lord, we believe. Please help us in the areas where we are not as strong (Mark 9:24b). Build us up, Lord!

Prayer:

Abba Father, thank you for your Word that tells us we are more than conquerors; we are the head and NOT the tail; we are above *only* and NOT beneath. Father, no matter how things look or seem, we know that our situation has nothing to do with our relationship and thoughts of you. We thank you for your unconditional love, unmerited favor, unspeakable joy, overflowing grace, mercies that are new every morning, strength made perfect in our weakness, peace that goes above and beyond our understanding, being in our right mind, and having the activity of our limbs. Thank you for never leaving nor forsaking us, for forgiving us and throwing our sins into the sea of forgetfulness. Thank you for making ways out of no way, opening doors and closing others. Thank you for hope and for help, for healing and even for holding us. And when this life on earth is completed, we know we have a greater home in heaven with you. Help us to reach our ordained destiny. In Jesus name. Amen.

Day THREE Topic: Ascension

Scripture:

> "But they that wait upon the Lord shall renew their strength; they shall mount up with wings as eagles; they shall run, and not be weary; and they shall walk, and not faint."
>
> Isaiah 40:31 KJV

Keywords: Wait. Renew. Strength.

Message:

There are times when we are up for the battle and there are times when we want to retreat …retreat, but not surrender. We need to rest sometimes, we need pouring into, and we need revival and/or restoration. Reenergized. There is no part of life outside of salvation worth returning to. Repeating that for emphasis: There is no part of life outside of salvation worth returning to. But there are times when we must sit at His feet, go into our closets, or lay flat on our faces; whatever it takes to hear from the Lord or gain direction for our personal situations. And the awesome thing about it is our Lord is nearby, waiting and wanting to care for us. He said His strength is made perfect in our weakness. So when we've given out, He's operating in full power to restore and renew. Nothing is too hard for God. And like Arnold, we can say: I'll be back!

Not only can the Lord sustain us, but He can carry us forward with power. This scripture says we will mount up with wings as eagles. There is no creature more powerful than the soaring eagle. He is strong and confident. Rising high above everything to the point where he can glide through the air with ease. So, after we've meditated on the Word, memorized it & digested it, we're ready to apply it. We can now move forward with a newness, a fresh anointing of strength and confidence. Ready to take flight. Rising to new heights.

Don't give up. Just wait on the Lord. Don't know what to do, where to turn? Just stand: keep doing what you're doing until you know to do differently, keep praying for direction, expect change, and be ready to act on the Word that is received. Rest and feast for a season, because in due time, you will be renewed!

Prayer:

Heavenly Father, we thank you for resurrection power. Because Jesus conquered everything we would or could encounter – including the grave – we can get up, walk away from, overcome, or walk through the fire and not even smell of smoke. Nothing shall by any means be able to harm us. Help us, Lord, to wait. Help our timing to line up with yours. Help us to rest and be assured that you are working on our behalf. You are coming to our rescue; we will NOT go under. We love you and we will give you all the praise, honor and glory. In Jesus name. Amen.

Day FOUR Topic: Deep Roots

Pastel drawing by Joanna M. Reynolds

Scripture:

"And he [we] shall be like a tree planted by the rivers of water, that bringeth forth his fruit in his season; his leaf also shall not wither, and whatsoever he [we] doeth shall prosper."

Psalms 1:3 KJV

Keywords: Tree. Planted. His [or Hers]. Prosper.

Message:

Take a look at Jeremiah 17:8 (KJV and MSG versions). Both verses make me smile. I get excited and humbled at the same time when I consider a tree. Awestruck. Takes me to the very essence of God. There's no explanation for a tree's life, characteristics, physical appearance, mere existence, other than God.

The Word tells us that when we delight and desire in the Lord and his precepts: instructions and teachings of God, and we habitually meditate by day and night on His Word, then we are compared to trees. And not just any tree. But those planted near rivers of water, their source, where the roots run deep because everything they need is near. Our source is Jesus. That sure foundation. Jesus. The *real* Rock. You may sway or bend, but you'll not break. Hold on through the storms, rains, droughts and the pain. The sun will shine again. And like that resting tree comes to life in his season with full blooms and grows bigger and taller and even greener than before – You, too, will go forth with greater works to produce greater things.

Prayer:

God Almighty, thank you for being our ever-present help: Comforter, Healer, Strong Tower, Provider, Peace, the Good Shepherd. Father, we thank you for strength in unity. We are touching and agreeing for each other's breakthrough and we are thankful that you are in our midst. (Matthew 18:19-20). We believe your Word that tells us a 3-fold cord is hard to brake. (Ecclesiastes 4:12) Thank you, Jesus, for interceding on our behalf. (Romans 8:34) Thank you, Holy Spirit, for bringing things to our remembrance. (John 14:26). Thank you God for your great sacrifice of love, for leading, guiding and directing us. We know that our experiences shape us into the persons you'd have us be. And because of the power in the blood (of Jesus) running deep within our soul, we continue to stand with strengthened faith. Forever grateful. Eternally yours. In the precious name of Jesus we pray. Amen.

Day FIVE Topic: Change Is Gonna Come!

Scripture:

> "Have not I commanded thee? Be strong and of a good courage; be not afraid, neither be though dismayed: for the Lord thy God is with thee withersoever thou goest."
>
> Joshua 1:9 KJV

Keywords: Commanded. Strength. Courage.

Message:

Change brings about new things or a difference in the current. Change invokes various emotions such as excitement, fear, doubt, and stress. Change can happen in a moment, overnight or in a day's time. It can also take weeks, months or even years. Some change you can plan for; some you have no control over. Change can be in circumstances or surroundings ... And some change takes place internally. It can be withIN us or happen TO us. Just before change hits, our hearts may beat as if it's coming out of our chest; we may cry (joy or pain), laugh or shake our heads in disbelief; our palms or forehead may sweat; and our minds may race: is this really happening? Am I doing the right thing? Did I really hear from God? Did I even seek His will?

It takes strength and courage to embrace change. Know that God prepares us for change in various ways. He knows what's best for each of us. He knows where we are trying to go and where He wants to take us. He knows. Our dilemma is that we don't. Sometimes we have no idea. We try to trust; keep your faith strong. Sometimes it'll take everything we have just to hold on, period. And in those times, especially if we have sought His guidance, He wants us to hold Him to His word. Try Him and see. Jesus said: In the world you shall have tribulation: but be of good cheer; I have overcome the world. (John 16:33 KJV) Additionally read Ephesians 6:10-18.

Prayer:

Father, help us to know that when things don't happen as we have planned or pictured in our mind, you're still working on our behalf. Your plan was different from ours. As we take steps to move forward, help us to realize that it is a faith walk. We know that we can do nothing on our own – we lean and depend on You. Our life is in your hands. If change is on the horizon, there is a reason for the shifting. There is something better for us and you'll guide us to whatever that is, at the appointed time. Help us to be obedient with our ears tuned to you. Help us to continue to seek your will. We're not sitting with our hands out. We understand that there is still work to be done. Help us to go with strength and courage. Help us to speak with clarity and authority. And when/if we are knocked to our knees, help us to realize that even there is where you would have us. And victory is still ours. We continue to lift each other up and bless the name of our Lord. We are strong and courageous because of Jesus. And in His name we do pray. Amen.

Day SIX Topic: Against the Odds

Scripture:

> No weapon that is formed against thee shall prosper, and every tongue that shall rise against thee in judgment thou shalt condemn. This is the heritage of the servants of the Lord, and their righteousness is of me, saith the Lord."
> Isaiah 54:17KJV …
> but *PLEASE* also read this in MSG for full effects. ☺

Keywords: Weapon. Against. Heritage.

Message:

The fact that you have to use a weapon signifies there is a difference of opinion, a struggle or challenge of some kind. Think about the different weapons that are used in the world today. And then if we go spiritual, think about the various weapons available there, too. This is a mean, cruel world and people will do (and say) about anything. We know there are physical battles, but the battle that we are in daily is not physical.

As Christians we have to remember that we have weapons that are to be used for our protection and well-being, also. Some of our weapons are trust, hope, prayer, praise, sometimes even laughter. The Word of God is the greatest! It helps equip us with whatever is needed to stand. … Because ultimately the battle is not ours, it's the Lord's. And our victory is assured.

This scripture tells us that nothing will come of the weapons that are formed against us. It does not say that weapons will not be formed — but the weapons that are formed will not be able to prosper (it won't succeed) — in other words, they will fail. And the Word even adds that because we belong to God, we should EXPECT all things to work out for the best. It is a decree, not a plea. We can trust it because the Lord said it.

I encourage you to get into the Word for there we find encouragement, instruction, discipline, strength, comfort, protection, peace and guidance for any and everything we are faced with. It is our heritage from our Heavenly Father.

Prayer:

Our Father which art in heaven, Hallowed be thou name. Thy kingdom come. Thy will be done in earth, as it is in heaven. Father, thank you so much for your written Word that is powerful and assuring. We thank You for being our shield, for watching over us, and for taking care of us. Help us to rise above the odds, go against the grain, stand firm, speak up, and do the right thing. And with bold faith we can even go into a lion's den without fear. We bring our petitions to You, asking, believing and expecting to receive. Increase our desire to study your Word to learn more about You, your will and plan for our lives. Thank you for the blessed assurance in salvation. We are washed in the blood of Jesus; now heirs of God through Christ. In Jesus name we pray. Amen.

Day SEVEN Topic: Blessed Assurance

Scripture:

> "For thus saith the Lord God …in quietness and in confidence shall be your strength."
>
> Isaiah 30:15 KJV

Keywords: Quietness. Confidence. Strength.

Message:

Wrapping up, I thought we'd take a look at the scripture text of the devotional title. In some way it doesn't seem like a natural fit. Quietness – Confidence – Strength. Who said you had to be loud in order to be acknowledged or recognized, to achieve or accomplish things yourself or to lead others? Where did the thought that quietness is a sign of weakness originate? What negative thoughts or behaviors are associated with a quiet manner?

What does the word "confidence" mean to you? If you give it some thought, I'm sure you'll agree that someone displaying confidence may not say a word, but your personal observations have brought you to the conclusion [that they are sure of themselves]. They aren't screaming: "I'm confident!" And they don't carry around signs and banners: "I am confident." Confidence in itself is a poise or assurance that speaks without words.

So if we heed the Word, we realize that Quietness + Confidence = Strength …because the Word said so, whether or not your supervisor, co-worker, family member or friend believes it. Let the nay-sayers know: I can show you better than I can tell you. Let us continue to live our lives and do everything as unto the Lord, and not unto men.

Prayer:

Father, we thank you that we can speak to you, for ourselves, at any moment (any time of the day or night). Our prayer can be audible to crowds, to our circle of friends/family, or only to ourselves. Our voice can even be as low as a whisper or a thought. And you can still hear and answer our prayers. God, we know you as Omniscient, Omnipresent, and Omnipotent. Thank you, God, for your gentle leading or nudges. Thank you for second (and multiple) chances. Thank you, Lord, for being more than enough. We thank you for providing our basic needs: food, clothes, shelter, jobs and transportation. Our confidence lies in You and we are eternally grateful for how You continue to shower us with Your blessings. In Jesus name we pray. Amen.

Closing

That's the end. I have enjoyed listening closely to my Father and writing these messages to share with you. God is faithful. He is so good. I am glad we proclaim Jesus as Lord and we are sealed until the day of redemption.

I hope that these devotionals have provided some encouragement, inspiration or positives of some sort. Did you have a favorite? Did any make a good discussion or study topic? Did any take you to the Word to find out more for yourself?

Prayerfully, your relationship with our Father and your confidence in and awareness of His love for you have been renewed and strengthened during the past week.

Keep praying. Pray for your family, your friends, your church, the lost and the hurting, and for our country. …All of America does not stand on "In God we trust." He is our source and if we stay focused, pray, believe and just live, we will be the church we were created to be and realize just how blessed we are.

Written (by Willette E. Mosby-Reynolds, inspired by God) in January 2016, with day seven falling on the birthdate of Ronnetta Monique Mosby, "my heart." Gone, but never forgotten.

Memoirs, Miracles and Other Moves of God

Table of Contents

First Faith Home

When I moved to Winston-Salem, Ronnetta, my then 2-year-old daughter, and I stayed at Fairchild Hills Apartments. I had inquired about a place there because it was based on your income. I did not know at the time that it was more or less "the projects." Where I came from in West Virginia, I knew nothing, or very little, about such housing communities.

We enjoyed our own place, made friends with neighbors and minded our own business. Other than work and church, we were at home. I would sit outside to watch Ronnetta as she played with the other kids in the neighborhood. I didn't know much about city life, but I knew I didn't trust it enough to let my baby play outside without my supervision. The kids thought (or sometimes said) that we were rich because Ronnetta had all kinds of toys.

We were a long way from rich and sometimes was left without dependable transportation. During these times, getting Ronnetta to and from daycare required strategy and stamina, as well as muscle and money. We would catch the bus that would take us closest to the center, walk the short distance to her daycare and once signed in, take her to her classroom. Then I would head off on my trek across several streets to catch another bus (the previous ran hourly) in order to get to work on time. The return trip was a little easier, but more costly. I would catch the bus to get off near the center, pickup Ronnetta and we would get a taxi to take us home. The city buses didn't run after six in the evening going in the direction of our apartment.

We still traveled back to West Virginia for Easter and Christmas. And one year right after Christmas, someone tried to break into our apartment. I think they were startled to learn that we had returned and didn't get past cutting a hole in the back screen to unlock that door. Well, that scare was enough to keep "Netta" close at night, so, if I needed to make any fast moves, she would be close by.

One day as I sat out front while she rode her big wheel, this little six-year-old boy told me how to roll and smoke a marijuana joint. I had already seen a man try his best to force this young woman into his car very much

25

against her will, and witnessed on several occasions children being locked outside their home while their parents did who knows what inside.

After almost two years, I decided that I had had enough and this was not the environment I wanted to raise my daughter. I talked it over with my heavenly Father. And without making any more on my job or receiving any other financial assistance, and without any concrete plans, I turned in my 30-day notice to vacate. I always took care of my home and felt this notice would justify the return of the security deposit that I paid when I first signed the lease to move in. I started checking the Classified's home rentals, praying for direction, and planning for my move.

As my 30 days continued to count down, I still had not secured another place for me and my daughter to live. Doors were closing. I would look at a house, take the key back and express an interest, only to find out it had already been taken; someone else paid the deposit first.

One evening after encountering another rejection, I just drove around looking and crying and talking to the Lord. I came upon this house with a "For Rent" sign in the yard. The neighborhood seemed nice enough. So I called to see if I could see the house.

The man on the other end seemed friendly and genuine. He asked when I would like to see it and we decided on that evening. I told him I had Bible Study, but could come immediately afterwards. He was willing to work with that. I was shown the house which I liked. I completed paperwork and paid the deposit.

By the time the 30 days had ran out, we were able to move into that home – all provided by the grace of God! Ronnetta and I now had a house, not an apartment, with two bedrooms, kitchen, dining room, bath, living room, nice front porch and yard and even a large backyard. There were children in the neighborhood and close by was a large fenced field that would be great for bike riding, kite flying, and any kind of play. Life was good. God is great!

The Engine that Could

I've had many cars in my lifetime. Some were clunkers. Some looked good, but still weren't dependable transportation. I have had a couple that I would call going above and beyond my expectations. And hard as it may seem, my little blue Chevy Chevette was one of those.

I remember that at one time we struggled with it because it had transmission issues. I took it to have it looked at, got an estimate for the repair, but drove it home. I didn't have the money for the repairs, so I just kept driving it and declaring that it was going to keep running. It got so bad that at times its pace was down to about a walk, not a drive. But I kept driving. It would get the kids to school and me to work – only by the grace of God. One day as we puttered toward the house, it kicked into gear and off we went. She [the Chevy] was saying I think I can, I think I can. Don't give up on me. I think I can.

On another occasion I mentioned to a friend the car issues and repair costs that I couldn't afford. She wrote me a check and I took it in to be repaired. When they called to say she was ready, the amount owed wasn't even as much as the amount of the gift I'd received. Praise God!

This little car served my whole family, and served us well. Extended family and all. I was the only one with a car at this time.

One weekend, we drove it to West Virginia to see my mom. Before returning home, we went grocery shopping there, so mom could be mom, know what I mean? There was a store in McDowell County with great prices and a variety of items that we could stock up on to stretch our money for a while. We purchased so much that we couldn't get the groceries in the little Chevette. So, of course, my mom just said to take her car home and we would switch off again in a couple of weeks when she came down to visit us. She had a Cadillac. We drove home and thanked God for His many blessings.

Even leaving the Chevette in West Virginia was not by chance. You see in the two weeks that we had Mom's car, it literally saved my family. One evening while sitting in that Cadillac outside the Wachovia building, my youngest sister had most of the family there waiting to pick me up from work. Well five o'clock came and I headed for the elevator and then out the door. I had gotten almost to the side of the car when I noticed, almost in slow motion, a city bus come down Fourth Street and then detoured straight our way.

I could not believe my eyes, and don't know if I even was thinking anything. But automatically, my smile at seeing my family waiting on me abruptly stopped and I'm sure my face expressed horror and I began to back up, back towards the steps to the front of the building. By this time, the bus took another sharp turn, but not before it caught the front driver's side corner of our car and began to push our car and we pushed another car backwards until everything stopped.

My youngest bounced from the car and started to run away from the crash. Guess it was shock or reflex. I caught her, held her close and kept repeating: Thank you, God. Thank you, Lord. Thank you. I was thankful because I could have seen almost my whole family wiped out as I watched and not been able to do anything. There were lots of people involved, but I don't remember any of them being seriously injured. My sister had a sore ribcage because the steering wheel was pushed back, my oldest niece had bruised knees, and my middle daughter had a bruise beneath one eye. But all in all, they were fine, to me anyway. There went my mom's car, but it had been our lifesaver for sure.

Back to the Chevette. After this accident, we had weeks and weeks of visits to the chiropractor. And we would haul everyone into the Chevette for treatments each time. Sitting shoulder to shoulder with smaller kids in the back hatch. How many people can get into a Chevette? We were sure willing to find out.

Self-Sustaining

Relationships require lots of work. Maintaining relationships and taking care of home looks different for different people depending on their circumstances.

For our family, it was better to build on mom and daughters. After the realization that "yes, I can do this," I set out to give it my best shot because the only true failure is when you fail to try. I began to talk to my heavenly Father and ask for direction. What do I do, how do I do it, when should I do it?

One day after picking up the baby and returning home to my latchkey daughters, I found the middle child (about six years old) outside on the porch, in the cold. She hadn't been able to get in the house. So she had done her homework and fallen asleep there at the door. The older daughter (who would have been about 11) was in the house. Probably sleep, I can't remember. But after getting in and getting things situated, I cried because my girls needed stability. They still needed guidance and someone they could depend on. They needed me to be there.

I began to pray about it. I couldn't afford afterschool care as well as childcare for the baby. I had to work to take care of all of us. I was the breadwinner, the provider for our household. It was me or nothing. No child support or additional funds could be counted on.

I was pretty knowledgeable about the computer – many light years ago, though. I was educated. I knew some people. So I began to think about starting my own business. This kind of thinking was not popular with some people. So as I planned, I shared some things and kept other things to myself. Still consulting with my heavenly Father on a regular basis.

At the appointed time I did what some would consider crazy. I turned in my two-week notice where I was working as office manager of this small, private, non-profit agency. I was recently separated, with three children, and talking about working from home at my own business. Yes, it was a leap of faith. Philippians 4:13.

When I gave my written notice, my manager asked what was I going to do. I told her I planned to start my own business and work from home so I could be there for my girls. Her reply: So, you think that's going to take care of you all? Yes, I did. I was depending on God to see me through. And he did. Philippians 4:19.

I started Unlimited Word Processing Services and operated it many years. I would do word processing for individuals and other small businesses: created wedding invitations and programs, church bulletins, resumes, all kinds of newsletters; typed thesis or other school papers, trained others on Microsoft Office applications (their office or my home). I did bookkeeping, individual tax returns and prepared 1099 forms during tax season. I was even fortunate enough to help two different individuals get their work in print; I typed their manuscripts that were later published. It was really a lucrative experience.

Whenever my business did not keep me busy enough to pay the bills, I would work temporary assignments. Those assignments could be whatever I requested: short-term, day, week, etc. I had some offices who would request no one but me to fill in for their administrative assistants when they were on vacation, or out of the office for various reasons. And during some of these assignments, I would be offered employment or asked what I'd like to be doing. So these were opportunities to let them know about my business and services I offered through it.

I enjoyed it so much that one day my baby said she was ready to go to school. I retorted quite fast: I ain't ready to go back to work (meaning not ready for the 9-to-5 jobs). But then after thinking over it a day or two, I asked: "God, is it time for me to return to the workforce?" He had allowed me the blessed opportunity to stay home with my baby for two years, until she was of age to start pre-school. She benefited almost 24/7, but so did the other two. I could see them off to school each morning, was there when they returned home, and could be more active in their school life: attending programs, having lunch with them, or whatever. I was blessed to be able to make sure my girls had the foundation and the start they needed to grow to be settled, confident, able-bodied, capable young ladies. And the means to this accomplishment was found within my house, and within myself, to proficiently provide for my family and still be a constant part of their day. My bills were paid and no creditors hounded me during this time. (2 Kings 4:1-7)

Fighting for My Angel

I could finally exhale! Our house could finally be a home. No more arguing or hostile situations, no more confusion! One of my girls had even made the comment that we were all happier, now.

Did I say "no more confusion?" Just when I thought things would settle down a little, my youngest daughter, Jazmyn, seemed awfully fussy or resistant whenever it came time to go to church.

At this time, I was working part-time at my church as the secretary, and was permitted to bring my three-year-old along with me each day. It was normally no big deal getting out each weekday for the 3-4 hours of office work and back in time to greet the older two girls when they arrived from school. Now, I was noticing that there were times that Jazmyn would become cranky and sometimes just down right defiant. I started to pay closer attention to these outbursts to try to pinpoint the cause.

Let me go back a minute. My husband used to ask me over and over if I believed in witchcraft, satanic powers, demons and such. At first I just brushed him off; these were things I'd never really thought about, so I really didn't know what I believed regarding them. The more I was asked, the more thought I put into it. And one day I replied that "well, yes, I know there is good and bad, there is a devil and there is a God. And, yes, there might be evil powers, but my faith is in God and I believe He has all powers. So it was still not a concern of mine." Well I learned in time that my husband believed in roots and palm readers …and in the Lord.

But back to this story. Jazmyn's behavior was getting worse, she was beginning to object more and more. My other two girls even noticed her strange behavior on Sundays. And as it continued, I mentioned it to my sister and even to my mom.

All of us were rooted and grounded in God, Jesus was Lord, and we believed in praying about any and every thing. My sister, Wawona, always said I would anoint anything. Well after we talked about it, we thought maybe it was a demonic spirit. It was so out of character for little Jazmyn, "my angel" as I lovingly call her. Otherwise, I would have disciplined her for that bad behavior for sure.

31

I had decided to anoint everything as we got ready for church this particular Sunday. My mom just happened to be visiting for the weekend. I had laid out Jazmyn's clothes and had her bath ready. The other two girls were now getting dressed and all was well. I anointed her dress, socks, shoes and bath water. I bathed her and started to dress her. She became more and more unruly with each step of this process.

As we wrestled there on the couch to get her clothes on, the girls were in their rooms and my mom was also getting ready in that part of the house. I was not quite sure what to expect from Jaz. My mom came up and tried to help. Netta and JoJo watched awhile. Then my mom said, "Well, I don't know what else to do." I could tell she was surprised, confused and concerned about what she was seeing. I was just glad that someone other than me and the girls was witnessing this; we were not crazy or making it up.

I told Mom to make sure that the other two girls were ready and asked if she would take them on to church. I would come on shortly. I asked her to tell my sister that if I wasn't there by the time they called for the announcements, which I did as part of my secretarial responsibilities, for her to read them for me. She and I did stuff like that for each other lots of times; guess it didn't help that many people thought we were twins. My mom's faith wasn't where mine was at that time, and if you aren't able to lock hands in agreement, sometimes it's better to stand [in the full power of the Lord] alone.

Once everyone was out of the house, I fought to put Jazmyn's shoes on. Now, remind you, this is a three-year-old baby girl and at this time she has the strength [seemingly] of several men. I sat on her and tried to hold her still. I turned her this way and that way. But try as I may, I could not get those shoes on her feet. I got off her and I sat at her feet.

I looked her dead in the face, and I started speaking to that spirit in her. I told satan that I rebuked him in the name of Jesus! I told him he would NOT take my baby and she was covered in the blood of Jesus! As soon as I pled the blood, I could see her began to calm down. As soon as she was herself again, she said, "Mommy, where are my shoes?" I picked them little black shoes up, got them on her and we headed for the door. Satan was bound and cast out of my child AND my home! God's free spirit of love, peace and joy could now roam and dwell. The shoes were the seal.

I got to church just as they called for the announcements and all I said was satan had tried his best to keep me from getting there that morning, **but God** ...and the church went wild. ...I guess I should thank my ex for preparing me for this. Satan is defeated. God is exalted. And we are victorious!!!

Prayer Does Change Things

I really am not super-spiritual. So why couldn't I find something else to do with my lunch time. Every day for like two-three weeks straight, I'd find an empty office on my floor and there I'd spend the time reading my Bible and praying. Then one day, and on the same day, I received requests from two different friends asking me to pray for their marriages. Me!? God, don't they know I'm divorced? Before I responded to either, I tried contacting my pastor. No such luck. So I prayed. Then followed up with both.

Funny thing about prayer is that it is communication with you and God. So, while I could pray for both or neither, it really helps to know that they are also praying and that what we are praying is on the same page. What are we praying for? What do we want to see happen as a result of our prayers? What do we believe? It's an awesome privilege to have direct means of contacting our heavenly Father for ourselves, but the Word tells us there is much power in the prayer of agreement. If we can touch and agree, things can happen for both [all] of us. Matthew 18:18-20 MSG.

I attended the same church with one; I assumed we had the same or similar understanding. But the other was a co-worker; I knew little about the type of faith she might have. So, I asked her specifically what she believed and shared what I believed. Once we were okay with that pivotal point, I shared scriptures for us to meditate on in our private time and we came together for prayer during lunch time.

This went on for several weeks. Tears were shed, conversations were taking place; there was work to be done. Our faith was strong and we were serious. Nothing comes easy. How bad do you want what you want? Do you *know* what you really want? Keep working. Don't give up. We called some things out, rebuked, bound and cast out some stuff and we loosed some things, too. And we kept pushing [PUSH: pray until something happens]. Things began to happen. More tears were shed. God was moving on our behalf.

That was about 18 years ago, and this couple is still together today. Stronger than ever. The other marriage was dissolved and both remarried. Note: My pastor said this "assignment" was meant for me, not him. And that was the real reason for my preparation time with the Lord in the days leading up to my friends' requests.

Am I My Brother's Keeper?

Life cycles are hard to break. And like almost anything else, awareness is key. As parents, we try to raise our children to be productive adults. We must take lots of things into consideration as we strategize how best to do this. A lot of it is by trial and error. Some of it is instinct, and some of it assistance from role models, books, etc. My constant mentor or coach is God, as I often seek direction from the Word.

The reason my brother was even here in North Carolina was because I had asked him to come. And after being here for several years, he had established himself and even married at one point. He had held multiple jobs, always considered a hard worker and was probably the only person I know that seemed to really *love* what he was doing.

Just as he'd seem to get settled in with the new job, things would change. The more he worked the more money he made, the more money he made the more he would drink, the more he drank the less dependable he would be. This continued until that job was gone. And this was his reality, a cycle he couldn't seem to break. Because he could not get a handle on it, he would continue this downward spiral until he had lost everything. Sleeping in his truck, hanging out wherever, doing whatever to make it through day by day.

When he'd had enough, he would make his way to my house and crash until he was ready to face the world again. This scenario would repeat for some time before I concluded that I could no longer allow him in. He wasn't going to break the cycle. He didn't really want better for himself. As long as he could count on me to be there for him, he would not stand on his own feet. I was not really helping him.

I prayed and knew that if I wanted to teach my girls to be independent, productive adults, they needed to see that. I could not "take care of" my brother, but expect them to stand on their own. I could not tell them that the man is the head of the home and the provider, when my brother was living off of me.

One of the hardest conversations I have ever had was the day I had to tell my brother that he was not welcome to stay in my home – especially when I knew he had nowhere else to stay. I held that conversation in private with him and explained that I had what I had because I worked hard for it. He had no obligations, no children, nothing that should hold him back from having the same as I had or better. I couldn't preach to my girls that you had to work to eat, that it's important to keep a roof over your head, that hard work affords you a decent life with necessities and luxuries, accordingly. And then allow him to lay around the house all day, eat what we ate, sleep, shower, wash his clothes, watch tv (hogging it and being rude to my girls), etc. and he do nothing to contribute positively to the household.

Years went by and because we know blood is thicker than water (there is nothing like family) – and there is power in the blood of Jesus – healing and restoration took place. The road was rocky, lots of hills and valleys, lots of bad days, lots of uncertainty. And believe it or not, he even thanked me about five years later for putting him out. That was a turning point for him. You see up until that point I had really been an enabler. Now he was empowered to press forward.

Today my brother has been drug and alcohol free for more than eight years. We as a family celebrate this accomplishment with him. We're proud of him, thankful and happy for him. He maintains his own home, has his own transportation, and has lots to be proud of. He has even survived a heart attack.

Scriptural Reference: Genesis 4:9 / Deuteronomy 6:7 /1 Peter 5:7

Triple for Previous Losses

A new job, a brand new car and to top it off a new home. The year was 1999. And when God showers you with blessings like this, it really can blow your mind.

I was working for the same company, but was moving into a new position and would be making more money. And I'd not even been job hunting. The job had actually come to me. One day I had mentioned to a friend that I would like to eventually get into the training department. I had a training background but understood that trainers had to travel. And as long as my girls were young, I chose jobs that allowed me to spend consistent time with them. And I tried to maximize this time, by seeing to it that we had quality time together. About two weeks after making that comment, I received a phone call from another friend telling me about a position and inviting me to apply for it. I did and got that position.

The previous car that I had was a lemon in every sense of the word. Too bad it wasn't yellow. I literally took it back to the place I'd gotten it and explained to them that I needed something dependable. I was making payments on a car that was sitting in my drive way; it was not drivable for one reason or another. After reviewing my payment history and discussing the matter, I left the car dealership with a brand new car. Not a lot of bells and whistles, but it was mine, I could afford the payments, and it was first new car – I normally purchased used cars.

And if that wasn't enough, I purposed that I would move before another winter in the lease-to-own home we had lived in for about two years. I knew after year one that I did not want to purchase it. My heating bills were sky high and the house was still cold. And the landlord always took the cheapest way out for needed repairs.

House-hunting was kind of fun, exciting, and even emotional. We all had certain things we liked about each. Sometimes there was not agreement out of the choices. But when I saw this house, I knew it was the one. This would be our next home.

I completed the necessary paperwork, made an offer, which was accepted, and then the real process began. And you know there had to be a hitch. I received a call saying I needed more than I had for the closing/down payment. She told me to try to borrow the needed amount.

A coworker/friend asked what was I going to do. I said, "Nothing. If God gave me the house, He will work it out." I wasn't going to borrow that and then need to pay that back as well as pay my mortgage and other bills. Another two weeks went by. I didn't call. They didn't call. Then one day the phone rang and she said they were sending the packet in that day for review. We waited. The answer returned: Approved.

When I told my friend, who stood closely by my side throughout the process, that everything had been approved, she shared my excitement. She had witnessed, like I had, another move of God! We went outside and ran, circling the building as we praised and thanked our Lord and Savior, Jesus Christ!

You see the real reason for our praise was not just that I had been approved for the house, without saving or borrowing a dime more. I had tried other housing options (e.g. modular homes), but nothing had been approved. But God had blessed me to get this home that had everything we needed, in my current state.

My right now was a second chance to be a homeowner, to raise my girls in our home, to have some of the things so many others take for granted. My Lord had shut doors that didn't lead to His plan for me and then He opened it wide. I lost the first home I was buying in my divorce years earlier along with so many other possessions. Until marriage, I had good credit. After marriage, I had filed for bankruptcy in an attempt to have a new start. Even with that still on my credit, God said YES, so no one else could say no. (2 Chronicles 20:15 and 17 / Proverbs 30:5)

Faith Confession for [My] Children

Being a single parent is not something I took lightly. I wanted so much more for my girls. I wanted them to dream big; to do great things; to ask, seek and find awesome experiences throughout their life journey; to question the status quo; and to be leaders: grounded and rooted and not following any and everything. I would repeatedly tell them that you need to have a strong mind. You have to know what you believe in; where you stand. You can't just follow the crowd without direction. And hearing things like "everybody else is" doing this or going, did not work with me. I would respond, "I like being different."

The Word says we can do all things through Christ who strengthens us. I wanted them to know what the Bible says we have and to not be afraid to go after their heart's desires. So, I constantly prayed a faith confession over my girls. I confessed it, declaring it over and over until it was memorized and hid in my heart, and eventually I hoped to see the manifestation. My confession was not long and drawn out, but I felt it was direct, complete and to the point. Here it is:

"Father, thank you for choosing me to be a mother. Help me to raise my girls in a way that is pleasing to you. My children are disciples, taught of the Lord. Great is their peace and undisturbed composure. Thank you God that my children are for signs and wonders. They will do mighty and marvelous works for your name's sake. They are the head and not the tail. They are above only, and not beneath. Thank you God for the saved friends, teachers, administrators, and everyday people who will cross their paths. Thank you for the people and angels who will minister unto them and for those who my girls will minister to in return. Thank you, God, that they are blessed and highly favored!"

I prayed the Word because God says He honors His Word above His Name. Maybe you'll be able to identify the scriptures included. A few foundational verses are Matthew 7:11/Luke 11:13, Isaiah 54:13, Isaiah 8:18, Psalm 127:3, 1 John 5:14-15KJV and Deuteronomy 28:13. And if it ministers to you, feel free to make it your faith confession for your children as well.

Losing My Heart

When the state trooper told me that my daughter, Ronnetta, had been in a car accident and hadn't made it, I repeated over and over, "I trust you, Lord, help me to understand. God, I trust, you, please help me understand."

Ronnetta was my oldest daughter. She was my first born and the child I had prayed for more than 20 years earlier. She was my "Samuel." Like Hannah, I had prayed for a child and had vowed to bring her up in the ways of the Lord. I felt with a child, I could pour out my love unconditionally and that love would be returned to me. I could love with all my heart and soul and that love would always be mine. There was no fear of rejection or thoughts of separation. She was "my heart" and I was driven to teach her about the Lord, and about right and wrong. I would tell her things with full explanations and often showed her things in the Bible to prove that it was my responsibility to instruct her as I did. I consulted with my Father on a regular basis and often prayed that I would raise her (and my other girls) in a way pleasing to God. I was thankful that He had blessed me to be a mom and often tell my girls that "many people can love them, but nobody can love them like Mommy loves them!"

The year 2001 was a very trying year. Early in 2001, I'd turned a relationship over to the Lord and even then I'd said, "I trust you, Lord." I remember during the Thanksgiving service that year, I testified that 2001 had been a hellacious year for me, but even in the midst of all I'd been through, God would still get the glory!" I told of the time I ran as my praise, circling the sanctuary twice and as I tried to stop, my spirit was moved to run one more lap. Thinking it may be for my three girls, I was obedient and completed lap number three. Well, I believe it was the very next Sunday that my brother was in church and during the call to discipleship, he came forward to give his life to Christ. Those close to me knew that I'd been praying for that very thing for almost 10 years! So, once again, I stomped satan's head and God was glorified!

Lo and behold, the week after Thanksgiving, my 21-year-old daughter – a senior and honor student in college – dies in a car/school bus accident on her way to work! There are no words to describe the feelings or define the moments surrounding this tragic time for me and my family. I just know that I prayed for the parents of a young man, who had died and left his twin sister and family to mourn his loss. I prayed for them, but knew nothing else about them but what I'd read in the newspaper. And because of that, I knew people were praying for us and the prayers of many helped to sustain us in our time of need.

Not only did I know and trust the Lord, but Ronnetta knew and trusted the Lord, too. She was strongly rooted and grounded in her faith. She often wrote inspirational poetry and always included in her closing "inspired by God, written by Ronnetta Mosby."

One of Ronnetta's poems foretold of her destiny (The Journey) and immediately after the accident, her sister, Joanna, wrote a poem (Journey Completed) confirming this ordained time. So, the challenge for us was in facing it, dealing with it, and finding purpose to move on. Our explanation to the many who asked or perhaps even thought: how are you doing so well? Isaiah 40:28-31. God is faithful! He said He would never leave us, nor forsake us. He will not put more on us than we can bear. He'll fight our battles. He will keep us in perfect peace if we keep our mind stayed on Him. His strength is made perfect in our weakness. Yes, this is how **we** do it – God, we trust You … help us to understand. And years later, He continues to unveil His plan. Deuteronomy 30:19.

Setup for My Comeback

All things happen for a reason. And there is nothing like God's timing. There is also nothing that compares to losing a child. It truly is like a part of your heart is ripped out. A part of you dies with them. It is so surreal – it's not supposed to happen that way. That's not the design of the circle of life.

I was notified after losing my daughter that I would soon be displaced from where I had worked for the past six years. So, though there was no need for that job in the merged company, I would receive severance pay for a set time. Guess this announcement could have been looked at from two views. And if you know me, I try to find the positive. What better opportunity to have time away from work and all those responsibilities? Good timing, I'd say. I always felt my time there had been an assignment. So if it was time to leave, the assignment(s) had been completed. Right?

In the months prior to Ronnetta's passing, God had revealed to me in a dream something about an open door. Since I wasn't quite sure what that meant I tried to prepare my spirit to be receptive to open doors: new opportunities, beginnings, relationships … What did God mean by "open door?"

During the months following, the grief would take me on several roller coasters. Sometimes I was so weighted down I could hardly raise my hand. Other times I talked non-stop about Netta and fond memories. And yet other times, I'd seek quiet spots and sit, stair at her photos on the wall and cry. The mornings were particularly hard, for me.

I sought opportunities that kept me busy. One thing that helped me was mini projects. My mom and I took on a home improvement project of giving my den a facelift: paint, window treatments, bookshelves, the whole works. It was fun shopping for the various items. Something productive for us to do. Finished project: bright, airy, a new leaf.

Another project was gathering the things Netta had written in her short lifetime. Looking for and finding them, reading them, and typing them up with a purpose and vision. My girls and I had often talked of collaborating on a series of children's books together. We would do the writing and illustrations ourselves. We were all blessed with those talents and/or enjoyed doing those things. But now since Ronnetta was no longer with us, she'd not have the opportunity. My vision was to publish her works – for her. So my goal was to get her book published before her graduation date so that her classmates could have a copy of the book to remember her. Another project accomplished, ***Rising above the Odds*** was published in April 2002; graduation was in May.

Focusing on someone else or something else helped me; serving others helps to channel those energies in a positive way. So, during my time at home, I sent greeting cards to the sick and shut-in, others experiencing a loss, or cards just to cheer someone else who may not have family nearby.

One afternoon, I received a phone call from a former co-worker. He was a manager and said he had already given my name to a hiring manager who was seeking to fill a position, the same as I'd held before being displaced. But after thinking about it, he thought that maybe he should check with me to see if I was ready to return to work. We laughed and I told him I would think about it.

I returned to full-time employment four months after being displaced. And though I had tried, unsuccessfully, to push the start date out until after the July holiday, I returned to a job that was the same position title, working near some of the same people, but with a pay increase. Not bad. An open door? Under different circumstances, it could have been looked at like having four months of paid time off when I most needed it. I had been blessed to have time off to start my healing process without negatively impacting the finances my family still needed and depended on for our livelihood. God is awesome! (Jeremiah 29:11 / Deuteronomy 8:18 / Romans 8:28)

A Thorn in My Side

It was great to be back at work. Something to help fill my time, give me meaningful work to keep my mind occupied and a good way to stay connected to people in general. Guess maybe the assignment was not finished – or maybe I had another. Only God knew.

After only a week or so, I noticed that there seemed to be some resentment from some. I was experiencing conflict and couldn't identify the root cause. My work is an extension of me. I give of myself and like serving or making things easier for someone else. But try as I might, there seemed to be no pleasing some ladies there that I was to work closely with on this new job. Had I returned to work too soon?

This one co-worker kept trying to make me do things for her and mentioned that the previous person in my position had reported to her. That was not the direction I'd been given when I was hired, though my manager was actually located in another city. At times, I would get so upset with this one young lady that I'd react out of character; one day even turning my back to keep from responding to a comment she made. They began to treat me like I couldn't do anything correct and even told another manager that I would do things arbitrarily to their work. Others were beginning to pick-up on the chaos.

I mentioned the office friction to my sister and told her there'd been days when I just wanted to get my things and leave. I am not a quitter and normally would not have been thinking that way. But I questioned myself and thought: maybe I really had come back to work too soon. My sister said that maybe since God had mentioned the open door, that maybe it was time to leave. I quickly responded that "No, that was all Willette." I'd not asked Him anything [this time].

This acknowledgement soon brought me to my knees. And once I talked to my heavenly Father about this situation and asked what I was to do. He directed me and I followed. Immediately, I could see and feel a difference with the one. Once the other came out of her office to my cubicle and tried to make a false accusation against me, but that day my reaction was to smile. I realized I had not included her as I followed God's leading.

My manager was aware of the situation and told me to continue to do the right thing. I was sincerely surprised at how fast things began to happen. I learned that I had gotten the position that they had recommended a friend of theirs for; therefore, they didn't want me to succeed there. They didn't know me or care about my qualifications.

Sometimes we pray and ask God to remove the thorn, and His response may be that His grace is sufficient. (2 Corinthians 12:9) He has also said if we have faith and doubt not, we can say to the mountain, be thou removed and cast into the sea and it shall be done. (Matthew 21:21/Mark 11:23). When His work was completed with that situation, I was still there and they were no longer with the company. (2 Corinthians 9:8 / 2 Corinthians 2:12-14)

Graduation Celebrations

The year 2009 was set to have several celebrations. Joanna was receiving her undergraduate degree and Jazmyn was graduating from high school. And I had been talking about the possibility of early retirement, excited about the accomplishment of having them all successfully through high school, the first big step. The youngest had already told her high school counselor that if she went straight into college after graduation, she would be wasting my money. She may never know just how much I appreciated that candidness. And the Lord had blessed me to be able to help Joanna complete her college education without a lot of student loan debt. We were so thankful for it all!

I reflected on the adversity my girls had faced. Life had not been easy. But God had blessed me with beautiful, strong willed, intelligent, independent, determined young ladies, who continued to push on against all odds. They were God fearing girls who loved the Lord. They also cared about people. Three girls, raised in a single parent home [for the most part], all finished high school and none had experienced teen pregnancy and those related circumstances.

As a child, Jazmyn had been accident prone. So many accidents and incidents that I once commented that the ER staff were going to be so familiar with her that they would pull her charts when we entered the doors. When I was first hired at one company, I had to leave so often to tend to her that I was afraid I would not pass my probation period. She had experienced fingers smashed in a car door, having a big goose egg as the result of being hit in the head with a stick at preschool, falling while running and having gravel embedded in her forehead, falling out of a moving vehicle, and being bullied in school from third grade on. One of her lowest points came after being told by a high school counselor that she "looked anorexic." What in the world!? She wasn't, we're just a thin family. She had survived it all – and was stronger because of it.

When she fell out of my mom's car as a little girl, she was bruised and scarred from head to toe. She looked so bad that my mom would not allow her to look in any mirror while she tried to clean her up for the trip to the hospital. After the examination and all the tests in the ER, we learned that she had not broken any bones. She was so sore that she cried when I held her because it hurt. That night I anointed her and prayed all soreness would be removed and that the scars would not remain, especially those on her face. The next morning, the soreness was gone, and the healing began. Yes, it was a miracle that the soreness was gone overnight and today she has no scars from that accident. Praise God!

Joanna, as the middle child from the start who was thrust into the elder role by the early passing of her big sister, was often mild tempered, easy going and no trouble at all. This temperament was often tested in those adolescent years by family and peers. She remained true to her colors. She's always been a leader, not afraid to stand alone from the pack, and often looked up to as the voice of wisdom, sometimes even being referred to as "grandma" by her friends who often came to her for advice.

As she entered college, it seemed that her ambitious drive intensified as she took the role of "big sister" very seriously and tried to do things right for her little sister coming up behind her. Following her sister's lead, she continued to be named to the Dean's List. She once told me that she had tried, but that she could not make the straight A's that Netta made. I told her I didn't expect her to because she was not Netta, she was JoJo. I really loved all three of their individual personalities.

One thing was sure, if Ronnetta passed the torch, Joanna was making sure she caught it and didn't drop it. Ronnetta, who earned a full scholarship after her freshman year at the university, had received promises of great jobs once she graduated. And since she didn't live to see her graduation day, we will never know. But as graduation neared for Joanna, she wasn't quite sure what her next chapter would be; she did not have a promising job lined up and waiting for her. She didn't skip a beat, though. She eagerly focused on what would be her plan B.

I've mentioned Ronnetta's pending graduation maybe a couple of times previously. Well, the university acknowledged her scholarly accomplishments along with the person she was and her degree was awarded posthumously. I actually walked in the graduation ceremony in her place. That was almost harder than the actual funeral service. I sat zoned out feeling almost like an out-of-body experience …listening to all the other young people excitedly discussing parties celebrating this big day and their future, watching their excitement as they posed for pictures and smiled at the anticipation of having this all behind them. ...and I thought about all the things Netta would never have the opportunity to experience.

Fast-forward seven years later, and the milestone is still graduation, but this time for her sisters. The relevance of this year and these occasions had me happily anticipating their futures and anxiously thinking about what life without [daily responsibilities for] the girls would mean for me. Was I ready for the empty nest? Nope, not at all. But the fact that my girls were graduating, though at two different academic levels, was reason for celebration. God had seen us all through to these appointed times for this occasion.

Oh, and I did not take early retirement that year. My precious, Joanna, had so bluntly reminded me that they still needed my income, because for some time, I was the only one with a job. So that hasty decision was put on hold; a daydream, not yet reality.

The Few, the Proud

I firmly lived by the belief that "I can do all things through Christ which strengthens me." (Philippians 4:13) And I encouraged my girls to do the same. Footnote: Later in life, I questioned whether that was good or not. But that's another story.

As mother, single mother, of three small and/or petite sized girls, I never even considered that I would be concerned in any way about the military. Boy, was I ever wrong. A month before college graduation, I was informed by my middle daughter that she was going to be an officer in the U.S.M.C. The Marines! My little girl?!? Are you serious!?!

Joanna had already done the research and lots of legwork. She knew Marines were tough, disciplined and well respected. She admired their strength and courage. She prayed about it and her heavenly Father had said: Yes, you can be a military officer.

Now what? She trained hard and continued to talk to others to gather information. She was focused and dedicated. Joanna wanted to make a difference. She wanted to inspire and encourage other young ladies. She worked with the recruiting office there near her university and they submitted her paperwork for Officer Candidate School (OCS). She continued to train and her excitement grew as she waited for acceptance notification.

She wasn't prepared for the news from the recruitment office. Her application had not been accepted for the next OCS because the office had not submitted complete paperwork. Joanna was devastated! But she didn't give up. Okay so what do you do when your Plan B doesn't come through? You develop a Plan C.

Joanna sought other jobs in the interim, but continued to work toward the next round of OCS. God had assured her that she could be a military officer. And she had asked specifically to be a Marine Officer. She worked hard, sometimes working two part-time jobs. But even though she had held her hopes high, she again received a rejection notice. She had to chalk another one up to not having submitted on her behalf a completed package.

It seemed that having a college degree was not paying off. But she was working, so she tried not to complain. On one of the jobs, she had to work into the wee hours of the morning and regularly lift packages of 60 lbs. or more. Talking about manual labor. Then she landed a full-time position, which was a great accomplishment in itself considering the job market and local unemployment rates. She completed that training and had her own route. It was a little physical, too, and required early hours. But one day she explained to me that though she was grateful for the position, she was not happy with it. It was not what she wanted to do.

And just like God, without notice and without doing anything additional on her part, Joanna received notice that she had been accepted and would report for the fall/winter OCS. So October 2010 she was off to Quantico, VA for training. She had been delayed, but not denied. Now for the real strength and endurance tests.

There were 66 females, about eight women of color, in her class at the start of the session. Only 19 graduated. She was once told that they hadn't graduated a black female in some time; and they didn't see her as being the first. But this little 5'4" 125 lb. young lady had made it through and she was the lone black female. It wasn't easy, but it was worth it. And though she had not realized it at the time, the jobs she had between undergraduate graduation and OCS, had literally helped to condition her for OCS. (Philippians 1:6). College life had helped to discipline her and affirm her faith foundation. And the opposition she had experienced in high school had prepared her for times she needed to put on her tough skin, though we know she still has a soft side. Ronnetta often said what didn't kill you will make you stronger. Well, Joanna is one tough little cookie. I once told her she was superwoman and I think it stuck in her head.

Joanna was promoted to Captain in April of 2015. Jazmyn & I were able to fly out to San Diego, CA to attend that ceremony and actually pinned her (placing the appropriate bars on her uniform collar). She has deployed once, has been responsible for hundreds of Marines, is looked up to and respected by all levels, and has seen lots of the world. Joanna currently serves as the Recruitment Advertisement Officer for the Southeastern Region of the U.S. for the Marine Corps. She's serving her country, contributing to her community and still impacting lives. For her good and His glory.

Consoling a Friend

In 2 Corinthians 1:3-5, we learn that we are comforted by the Comforter, so that we in turn can comfort someone else.

Grief is a process and it's not a step-by-step process with a timeline from start to finish. Each person must realize they may jump from step-to-step, skipping some, repeating some, and approaching each differently and really in no particular order at all. The important thing to remember is feel whatever it is that you feel, when you feel it, but try not to get stuck, especially in those negative feelings. Try to move forward. Think about: What or who can help you? How can you find purpose and/or hope? What are the positives in a situation?

Some years later after a friend of mine also lost a child to sudden death, we often met for lunch to chat and cheer each other up. Most times she asked about the grief or healing process. We talked about our families and how different individuals grieved differently. We talked about hypothetical situations and how to cope or approach situations. One question was when would she be happy again or could she be happy, again? I answered that question with a question: What is happiness?

We had been friends for many years, but I tried to keep the conversation "normal" trying not to impose my spiritual beliefs; trying not to "talk Bible." I didn't want to scare her away, but was open to sharing my thoughts and feelings with her, especially if my experience could in some way help her through hers. And like most mothers, we all cherish the memories and yearn for opportunities to say our loved one's (gone too soon) name aloud or talk about them as if they are still here with us. So these times together were moments and lunches we both looked forward to.

Then she asked how was I doing as well as I was? What was my secret? I paused and searched for the right words and the right way to respond. That question I could not answer without talking about my Lord and Savior; I could not not quote some scripture as my "help." So, I smiled and said, the Word says that if we trust and keep our mind stayed on Him, He will keep us in perfect peace. His strength is made perfect in weakness. So if anything, I am a perfect example of weakness. I'd definitely turned everything over to Him; it was too much for little ole me. And lastly, I said, "Life is about choices and I literally choose LIFE. I am still surrounded by people who love me. I owe it to them to return their love and attention with my own towards them. I do not want to be stuck in a rut; always sad, down and out. Ronnetta would not want that for me, either. I chose to move forward with my life, to honor and remember her life, and to work with the expectation of seeing her again, one day." (Deuteronomy 30:19)

There are many memories and friends that could have been included here. And unfortunately, several who have also lost a child. I chose this one primarily because of the "choice" statement. It's a good way to close this chapter and this work. But it also leaves the door open for plenty of other memories to be created, miracles to be performed, and life to be lived.

"Now the God of hope fill you with all joy and peace
in believing that ye may abound in the hope, through the
power of the Holy Ghost."

(Romans 15:13 KJV)